T0030659

READY, SET, RUN!
21658
THE AMAZING NEW YORK CITY MARATHON
NYC marathon

NEW JERSEY
Staten Island
Upper NY Bay
Liberty Island
Ellis Island
N
W
E
S
START here
The Narrows
Governors Island
M
EAST
Verrazzano-Narrows Bridge
Brooklyn Bridge
Manhattan Bridge
4th AVE.
Lafayette Ave.
Lower NY Bay
BROOKLYN

HUDSON // RIVER

George
Washington →|
Bridge

FINISH LINE

↓

HA**TTAN**

✳ CENTRAL
PARK

Madison
Ave.
Bridge
↓

RIVER

5th AVE.

Ed Koch
Queensboro
Bridge

1st AVE.

RIVER

→

The

BRONX

HARLEM ↑

ROOSEVELT
ISLAND

Pulaski Bridge
↓

Willis
Ave.
Bridge

Berry St.
←

Rikers
Island

···g
Ave.

HALFWAY
POINT

QUEENS

✳ **The ROUTE** ✳

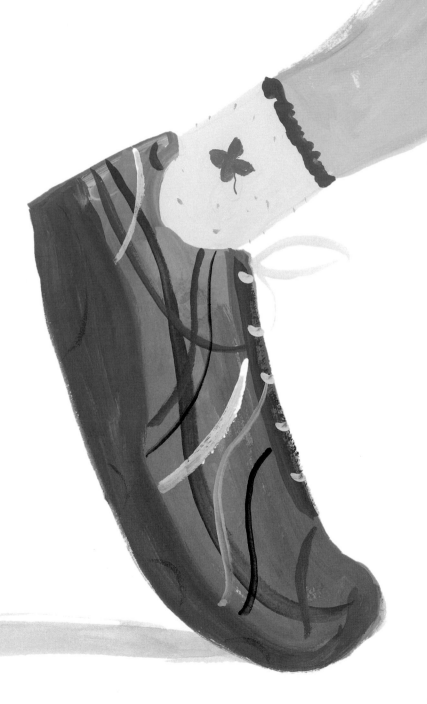

TO THE CITY I LOVE —L.K.

DEDICATED TO THE PEOPLE OF
NEW YORK CITY: THE RUNNERS,
THE WALKERS, THE STROLLERS,
AND THE DAWDLERS —J.H.

Text copyright © 2023 by Leslie A. Kimmelman
Jacket and interior illustrations copyright © 2023 by Jessie Hartland

All rights reserved. Published in the United States by Random House Studio, an imprint of
Random House Children's Books, a division of Penguin Random House LLC, New York.

Random House Studio with colophon is a trademark of Penguin Random House LLC.

Visit us on the Web! rhcbooks.com

Educators and librarians, for a variety of teaching tools, visit us at RHTeachersLibrarians.com

Library of Congress Cataloging-in-Publication Data is available upon request.
ISBN 978-0-593-43365-2 (trade) — ISBN 978-0-593-43366-9 (lib. bdg.)
ISBN 978-0-593-43367-6 (ebook)

The text of this book is set in 15-point Brandon Grotesque.
The illustrations were rendered in gouache.
Book design by Rachael Cole

MANUFACTURED IN CHINA
10 9 8 7 6 5 4 3 2 1
First Edition

Random House Children's Books supports the First Amendment
and celebrates the right to read.

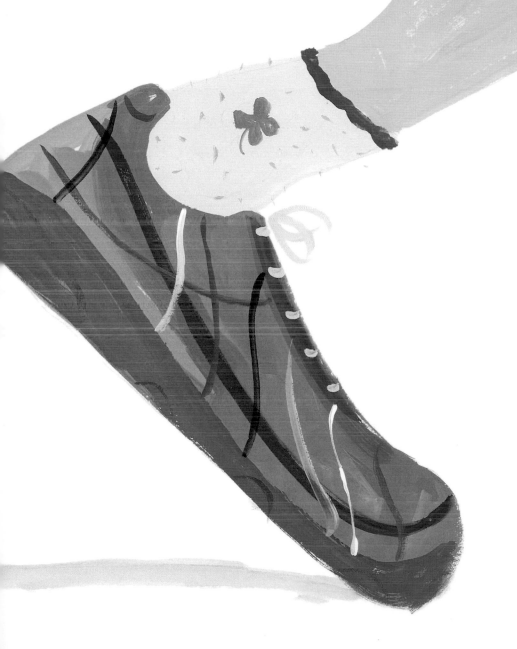

READY, SET, RUN!

THE AMAZING NEW YORK CITY MARATHON

WRITTEN BY
LESLIE KIMMELMAN

ILLUSTRATED BY
JESSIE HARTLAND

RANDOM HOUSE STUDIO NEW YORK

EXTRA! PEOPLE FROM MORE THAN 100 COUNTRIES RUN IN THE NEW YORK CITY MARATHON.

All over the world—
on city roads
and country lanes,
on beaches,
high in the mountains,
across fields
and through forests,
in sun, in rain, and late at night—
people get ready to race.

OCEAN

NEW YORK

It's a **BIG DEAL** to run in the New York City Marathon.

They make sure their running shoes fit.

They stretch.

They add some music to their playlist.

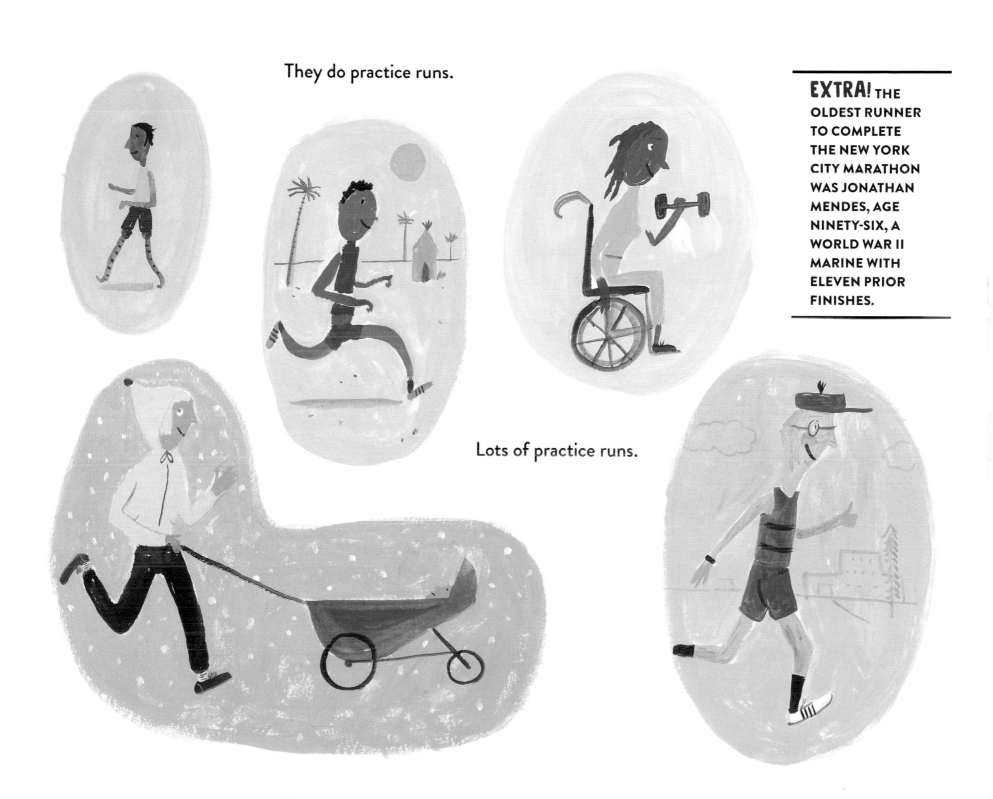

They do practice runs.

Lots of practice runs.

EXTRA! THE OLDEST RUNNER TO COMPLETE THE NEW YORK CITY MARATHON WAS JONATHAN MENDES, AGE NINETY-SIX, A WORLD WAR II MARINE WITH ELEVEN PRIOR FINISHES.

The New York City Marathon is held every year on the first Sunday in November.

Some runners already live in New York City.

EXTRA! THE YOUNGEST RACER TO FINISH THE MARATHON WAS WESLEY PAUL, AGE EIGHT, WHO FINISHED IN JUST OVER THREE HOURS IN 1977. NOW YOU MUST BE AT LEAST EIGHTEEN YEARS OLD TO RUN.

The others travel

by plane or train, in buses and cars.

or warm bubble baths.

It's the night before the marathon.
Runners take long showers

EXTRA! THE RACE HAS BEEN CANCELED ONLY TWICE. THE FIRST TIME WAS IN 2012, THE YEAR OF HURRICANE SANDY. RUNNERS PITCHED IN TO HELP CLEAN UP THE DAMAGE. IT WAS CANCELED AGAIN IN 2020 BECAUSE OF THE COVID-19 PANDEMIC.

Some eat big spaghetti dinners.

This runner has a lucky sweatband,

and that runner
has lucky socks.

Zzzz z z zzz

Everyone tries to get
a good night's sleep.

It's still dark
when runners make their way
to the starting area
on Staten Island.

What a colorful crowd!
People eat and drink,
use the bathrooms,
and visit the therapy pups.

One runner
even squeezes
in a quick nap.

undpoundpoundpoundpoundpoundpoundpoundpoundpoundpoundpoundpour

BOOM! The race begins.

poundpoundpoundpoundpoundpoundpoundpoundpoundpoundpoundpo

They jog and stretch
and toss the clothing they won't need on the ground.

The song "New York, New York"
blares its way through the crowd.

EXTRA! THE CLOTHING
(ABOUT TWENTY-SIX TONS!)
THAT RUNNERS LEAVE ON
THE GROUND IS COLLECTED
AND DONATED TO CHARITY.

ndpoundpoundpoundpoundpoundpoundpoundpoundpoundpoundpound

EXTRA! MANY RUNNERS WRITE THEIR NAMES ON THEIR
SHIRTS SO PEOPLE CAN CHEER THEM ON BY NAME!

undpoundpoundpoundpoundpoundpoundpoundpoundpoundpoundpou

Hello, Brooklyn!

Running really works up an appetite.
Here is what racers grab to eat and drink along their way:

bananas

water

sports drinks

pretzels

(more than 32,000 are eaten by runners on race day!)

EXTRA! THERE ARE FOOD AND WATER STATIONS, BATHROOM STATIONS, AND FIRST AID STATIONS ALL ALONG THE ROUTE OF THE MARATHON.

energy gels

gummy candies

orange slices

(watch out, they're sticky!)

and energy bars

When racers reach Queens, they've gone halfway. Hooray! And just as quickly as they arrived, they're heading back out again. The Ed Koch Queensboro Bridge is absolutely quiet except for the pounding of the runners' feet. Then suddenly . . .

keep GOING!

CIRCLE LINE

M

Manhattan

Island

GO MOM

EXTRA! SINCE 1979, A HIGH SCHOOL BAND STATIONED AT MILE 9 HAS PLAYED THE *ROCKY* THEME SONG AGAIN AND AGAIN UNTIL THE LAST RUNNERS HAVE GONE BY.

ROARRRRRRRRRRRRRRR!

Welcome to Manhattan!

The fastest runners are starting to break away.

HOUSEWARES

PIZZA

FIRST AVENUE

KITCHEN

HARDWARE

KNIVES

we have been trying to reach you about your extended WARRANTY

NONE of that!

PAINT TOOLS

EXTRA! ALMOST ALL OF THE FIFTY FASTEST MEN'S MARATHON TIMES ARE HELD BY RUNNERS FROM KENYA AND ETHIOPIA.

All racers are welcome:

 young

and old

jogglers

wheelchair racers

even Spider-Man!

Lots of people run to raise money for good causes.

Who's faster, police officers or firefighters?

Just as runners reach the Bronx, at about twenty miles, they hit "the wall." It's not really a wall!

The BRONX welcomes you!

C-town

Helados TROPICALES

El Barrio music center

COCI CRIO

MINDY, you're AWESOME!

RUN, RICK, RUN!

we have been trying to reach you about your extended warranty

GO CÉSAR!

It just means that everyone is very very VERY tired.
Some people slow down and walk for a while.

EXTRA! OFTEN JAPANESE DRUMMERS PLAY IN THE BRONX, TO URGE RUNNERS ON AT THE HARDEST PART OF THE RACE.

Back in Manhattan! The good news is that it's close to the finish line. The bad news is that it's UPHILL! But crowds are waving flags and screaming at the top of their lungs:

Keepgoingkeepgoingkeepgoingkeepgoingkeepgoing!

Central Park is waiting.

EXTRA! THE FIRST MARATHON WAS ORGANIZED BY FRED LEBOW, WHO WAS THE RACE DIRECTOR FOR MORE THAN TWENTY YEARS. THERE'S A STATUE OF HIM IN CENTRAL PARK, WHICH IS MOVED TO THE FINISH LINE EVERY YEAR ON RACE DAY.

Crossing the finish line is like flying.
The runners feel amazing.

TIME
2:37:03

NYC marathon

Proud.

Sore.

Tired.

Dazed—they've done it!

Three cheers for the winners!

FIRST
AID

Refresh!

EXTRA! NORWEGIAN RUNNER
GRETE WAITZ WON THE NEW YORK
CITY MARATHON NINE TIMES!

But *all* the runners are winners. So medals for everyone!

EXTRA! SINCE 1972, THE WINNERS' LEAFY CROWNS HAVE
BEEN HANDMADE BY THE SAME PERSON, JANE MUHRCKE.

The race is over, but the runners keep walking so their
muscles don't cramp and stiffen. Slowly, slowly, slowly,
they go their separate ways . . .

to hugs,

to dinner,

to a hot soak in a tub,

to sleep.

What a city!
What a day!
What an amazing race!

AUTHOR'S NOTE

Marathons—which are 26.2 miles long—are run in cities all around the world and in the Summer Olympics. I live and work in New York, so I chose to write about the New York City Marathon.

The first NYC Marathon was held in 1970; the route was a little more than four laps around Central Park. Paying a $1 entrance fee, 127 runners entered. Only 55 finished. Women were officially allowed to run two years later, in 1972. The six women were given a ten-minute head start, but when the starting gun went off, they sat down in protest. Ten minutes later, they began the race *with* the men.

These days, more than 50,000 runners cross the finish line each year, and the race goes through all five boroughs, or sections, of the city—Staten Island, Brooklyn, Queens, the Bronx, and Manhattan—and across five bridges.

There are too many racers for everyone to begin together, so there are different start times for different groups of runners. The first to go are the professional wheelchair racers at 8:00 a.m.; the last group of marathon runners takes off at 11:30. The fastest runners finish in slightly over two hours. The last runners may take ten or even twelve hours . . . but however long it takes, it's still a terrific accomplishment!

The roads are lined with millions of people watching and yelling encouragement. If you're in the city on Marathon Day, come out and cheer for the runners. One November, maybe you'll even run it yourself!

ACKNOWLEDGMENTS

My daughter, Natalie, who has a front-row view of the marathon on its Brooklyn leg, gave me the idea for this book. As always, her every suggestion made the book better. A big thank-you as well to Meaghan Burke, Mindy Brooks, and Rick Slocum for sharing so vividly their firsthand experiences running the NYC Marathon.   L.K.

Thanks to Dr. Julia McGuinness, MD, who answered my numerous questions about the experience. —J.H.

SELECTED SOURCES

New York Road Runners
    nyrr.org

Aisch, Gregor, and Ken Schwencke. "New York City Marathon in Six Charts." *New York Times,* Oct. 30, 2015.
    nytimes.com/interactive/2015/10/30/sports/new-york-marathon-in-six-charts.html?searchResultPosition=11

Barakat, Zena, Flora Lichtman, and Will Storey. "New York City Marathon, by the Numbers." *New York Times,* Nov. 1, 2013.
    nytimes.com/video/sports/100000002529991/new-york-city-marathon-by-the-numbers.html?searchResultPosition=6

Hirsch, George A. "It Was 50 Years Ago Today, the Marathon Came to New York to Stay." *New York Times,* Sept. 13, 2020.
    nytimes.com/2020/09/13/sports/new-york-city-marathon.html?searchResultPosition=4

Hughes, C. J. "Along the Route, Neighborhood Snapshots of New York's Progression." *New York Times,* Nov. 4, 2011.
    nytimes.com/2011/11/05/sports/marathon-route-gives-snapshots-of-change-in-new-york.html?searchResultPosition=5

Kern, Colin. "The Wreaths for the Marathon Winners Come from My Grandmother's Backyard." *New York Times,* Oct. 28, 2019.
    nytimes.com/2019/10/28/nyregion/nyc-marathon-wreaths.html?searchResultPosition=1

"The New York City Marathon: A Poem in Sights and Sounds." *New York Times,* Oct. 28, 2014.
    nytimes.com/interactive/2014/10/28/sports/marathon-videos.html?searchResultPosition=1